Fuck That Shit

The Garden and Flower Swear Words

Adult Coloring Book

By

S.B. Nozaz

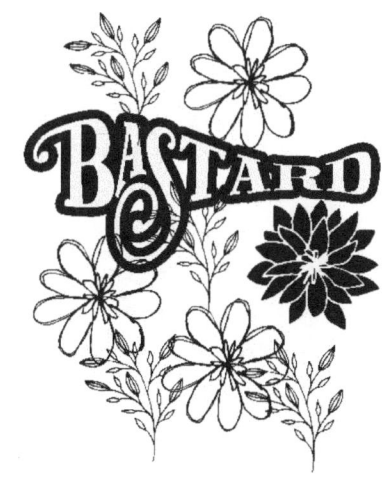

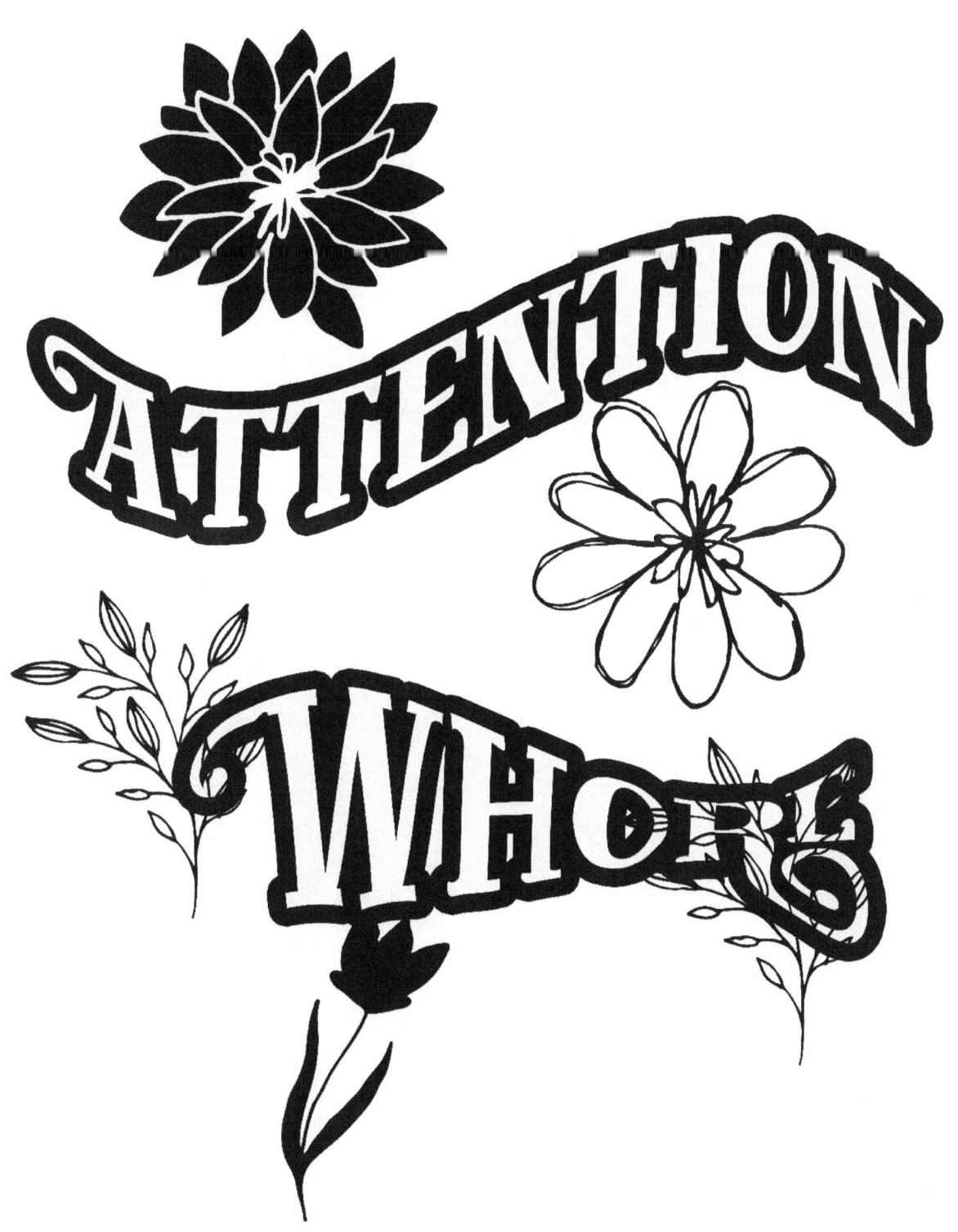

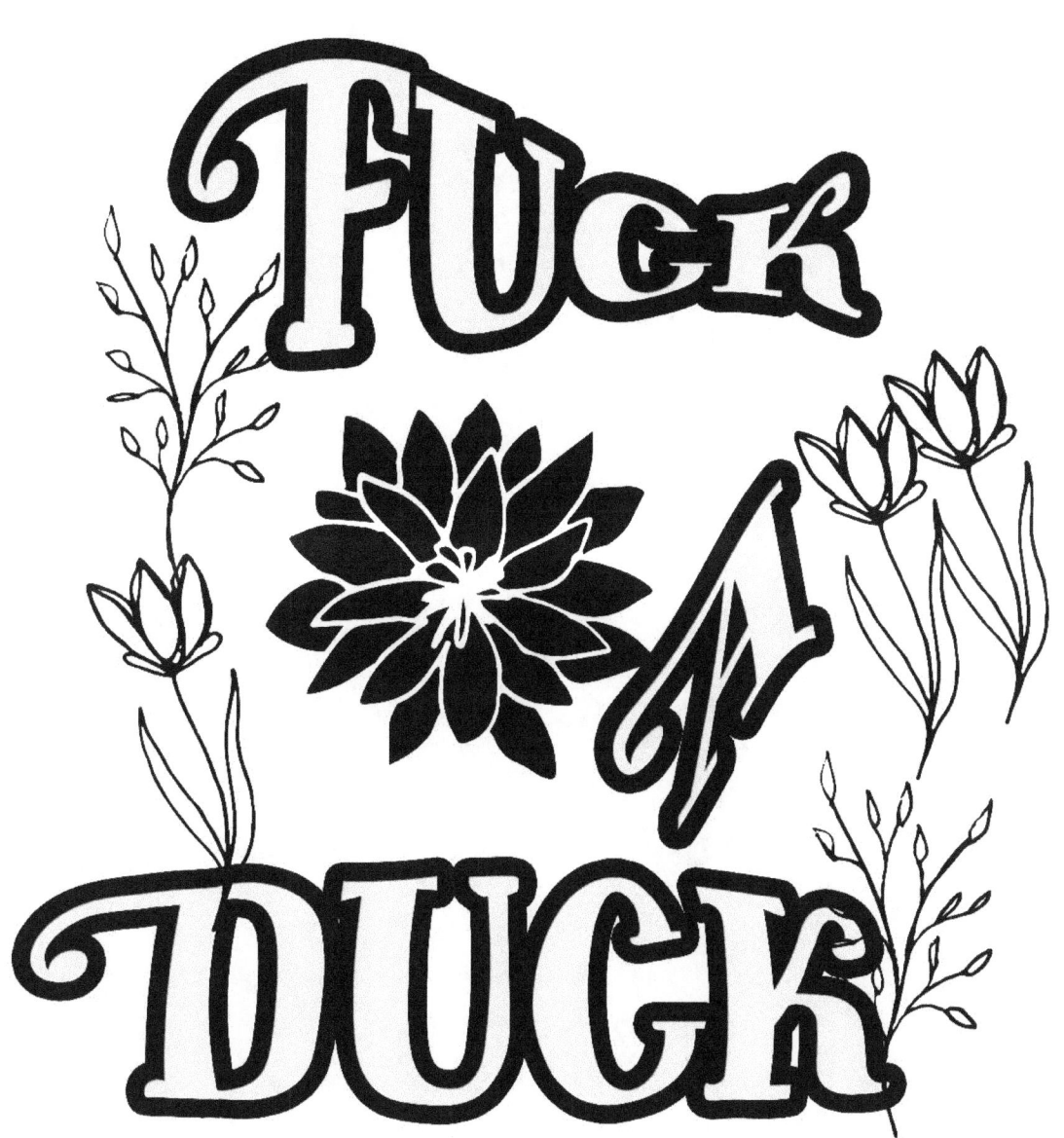

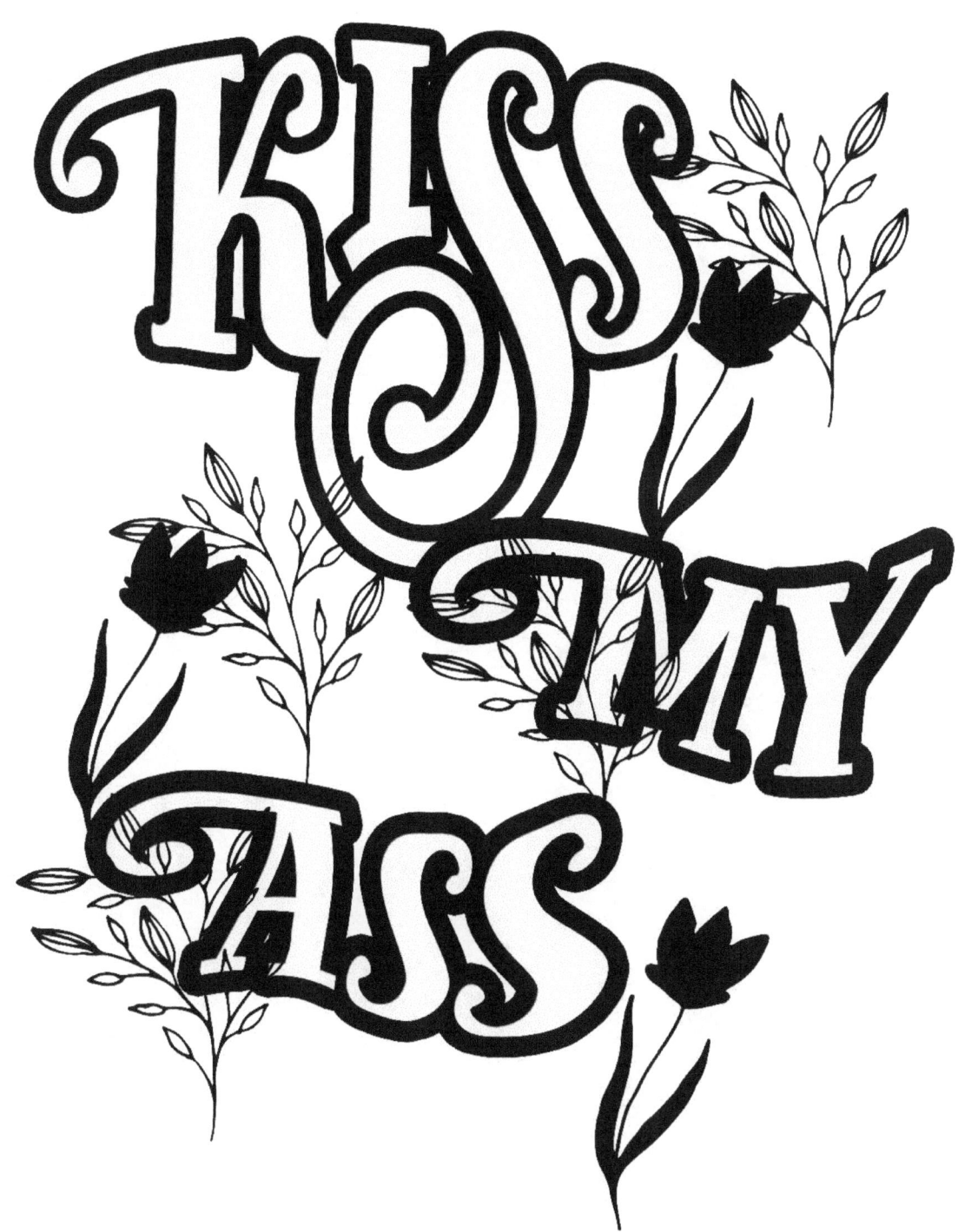

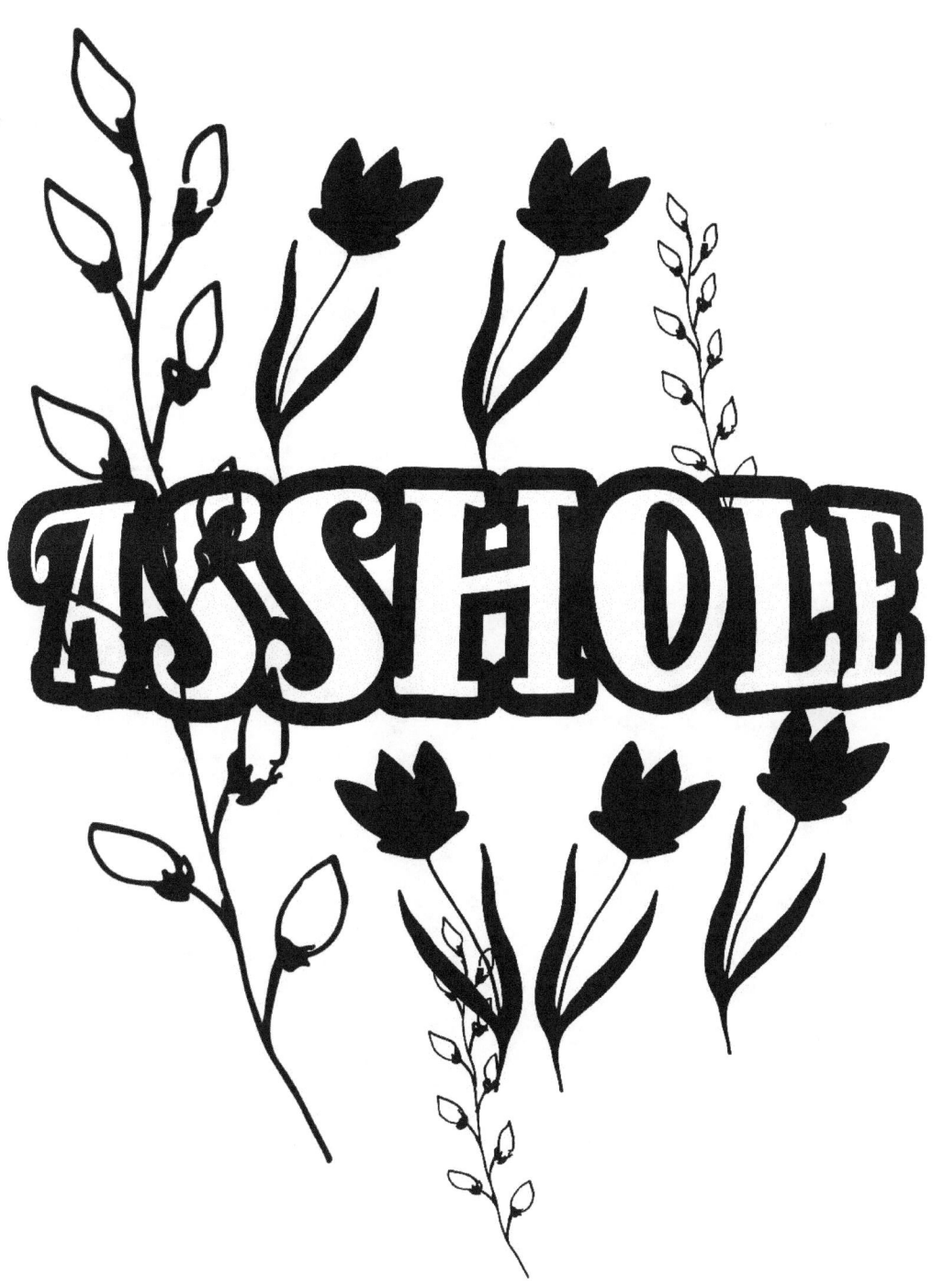

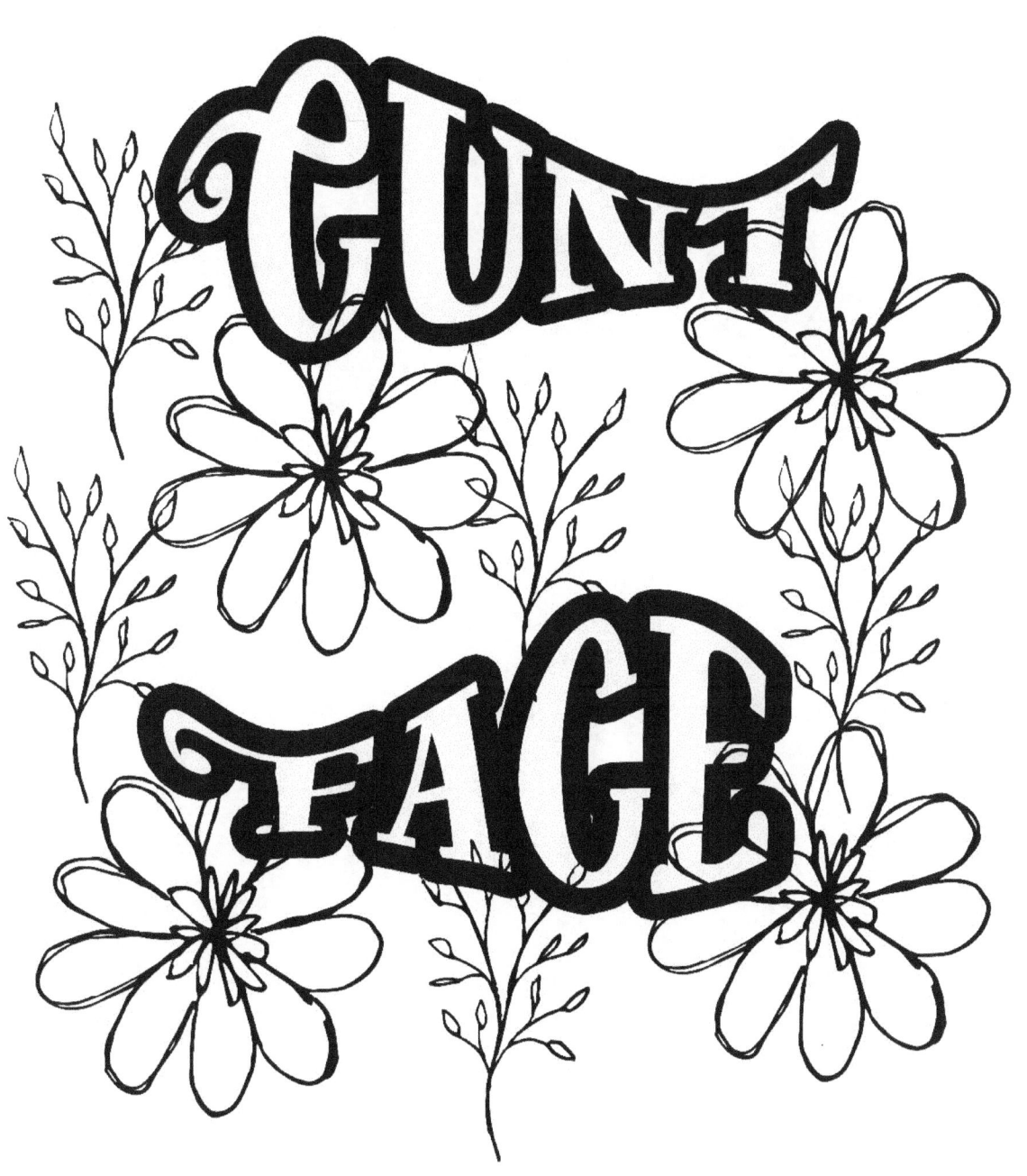

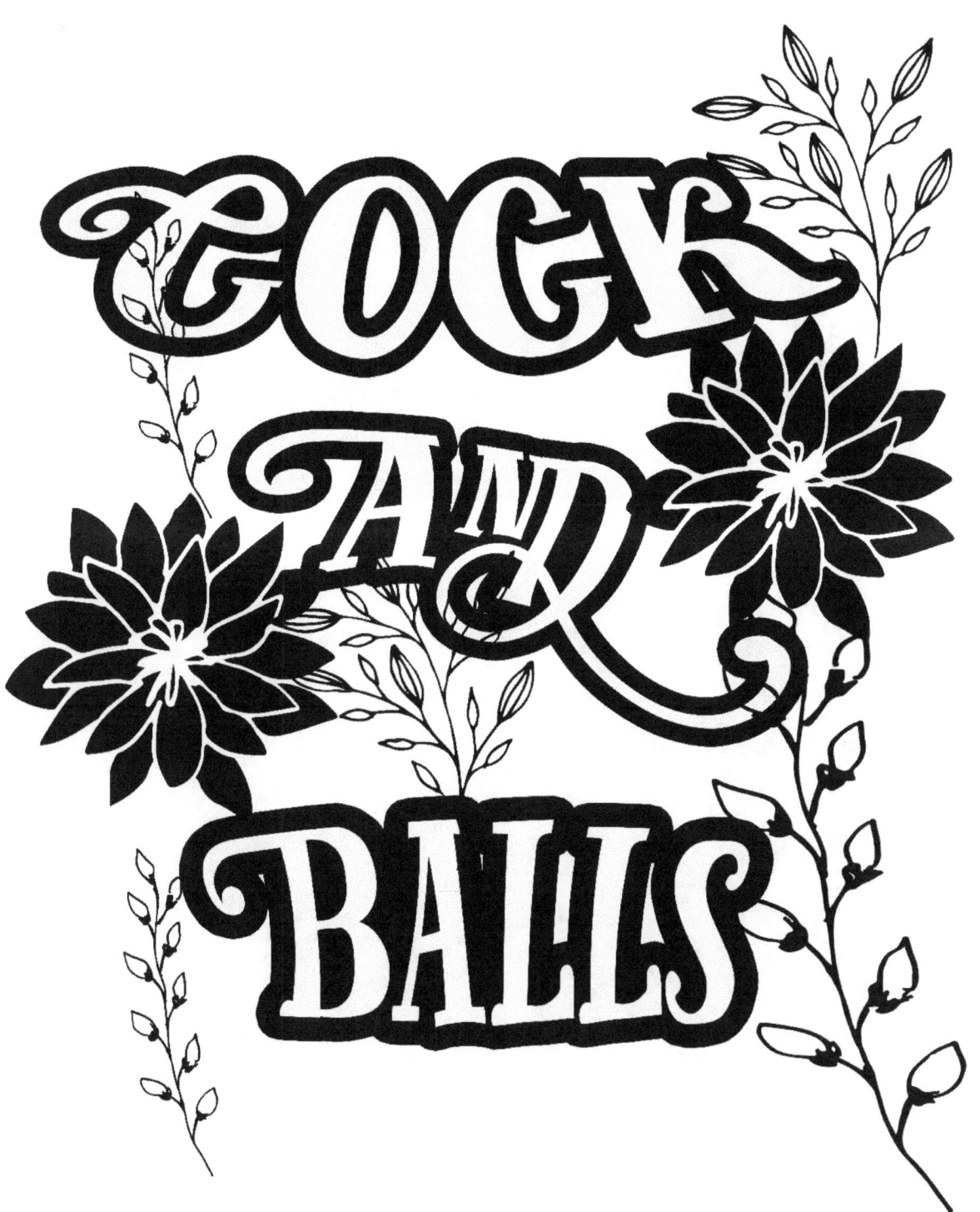

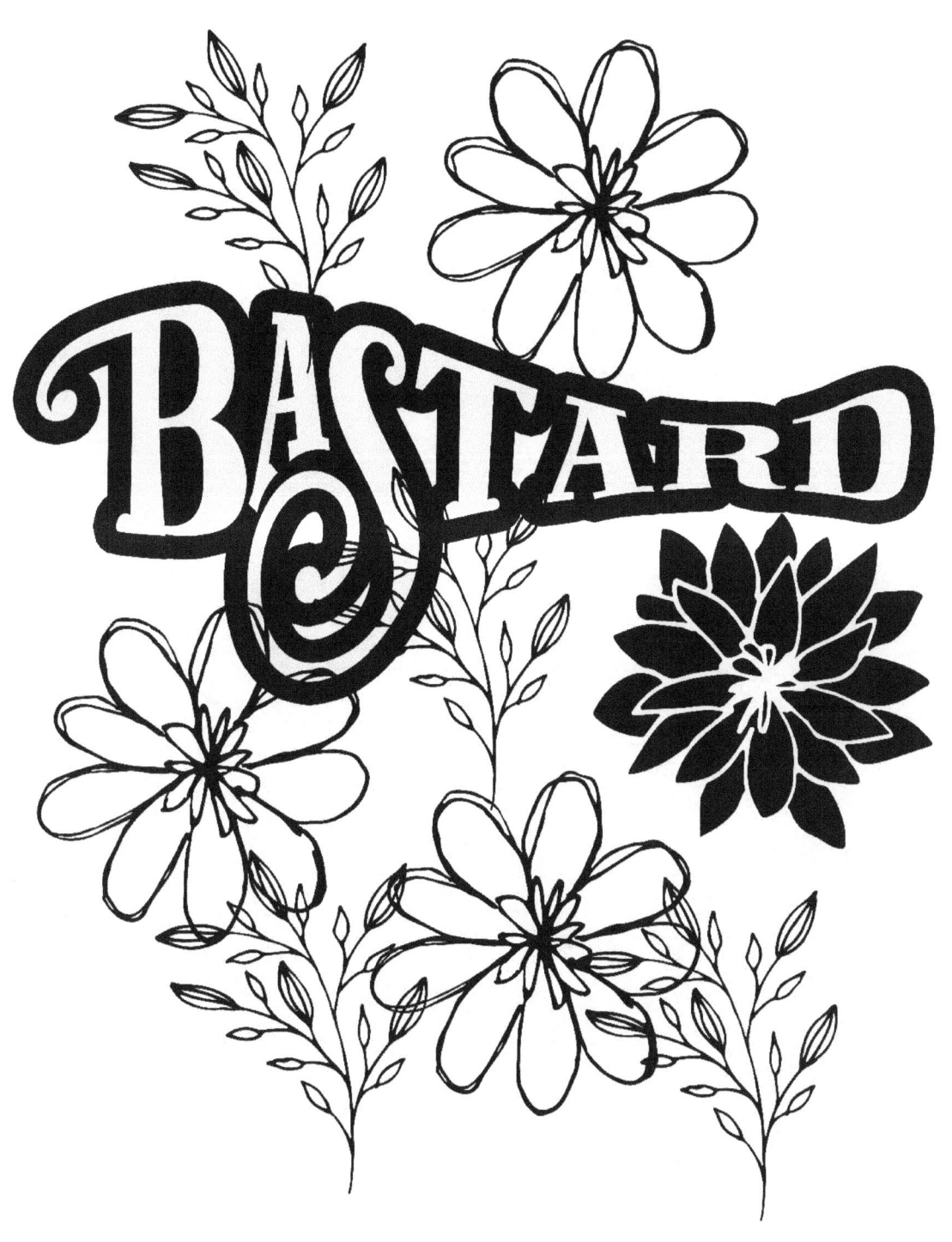

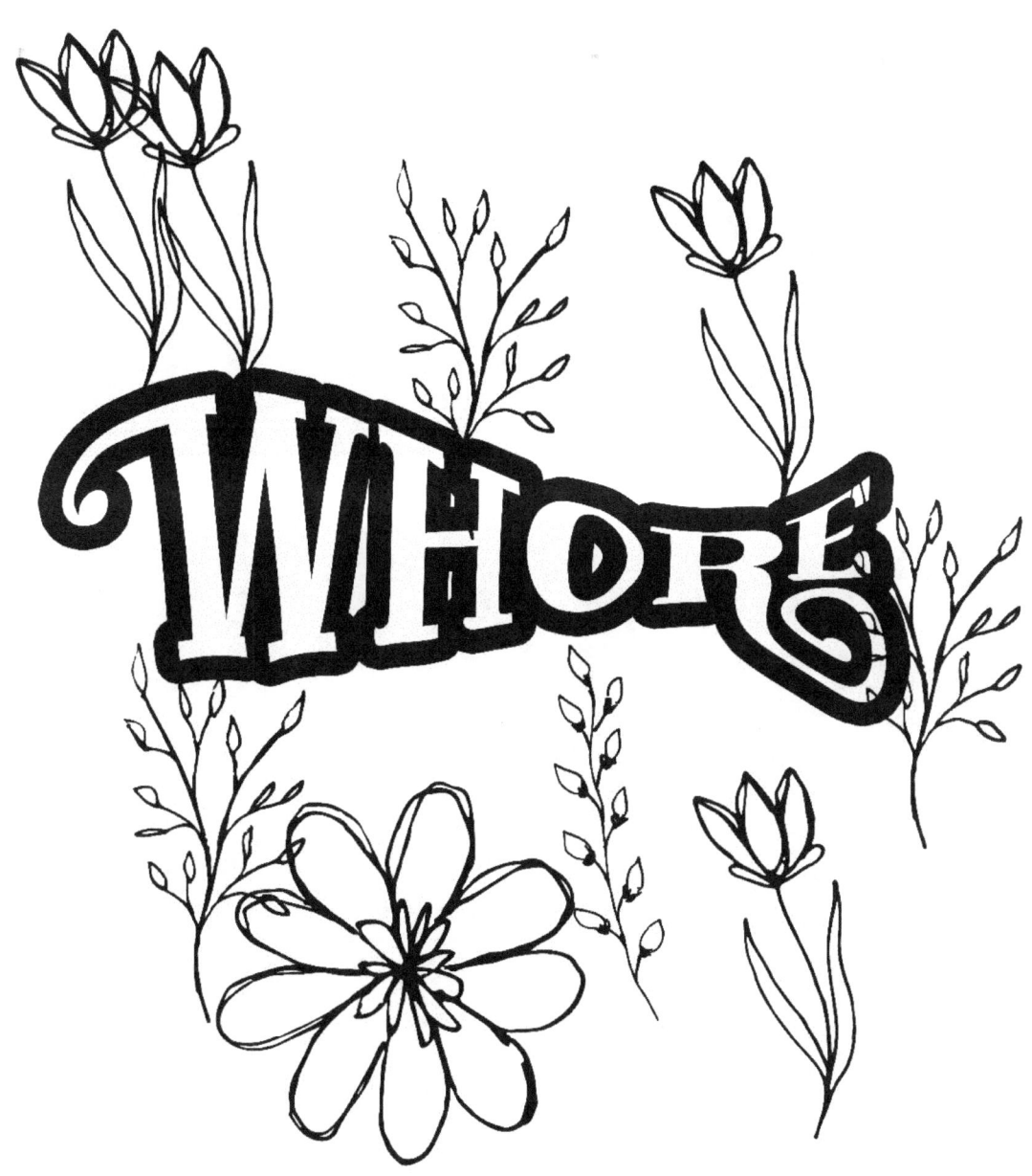

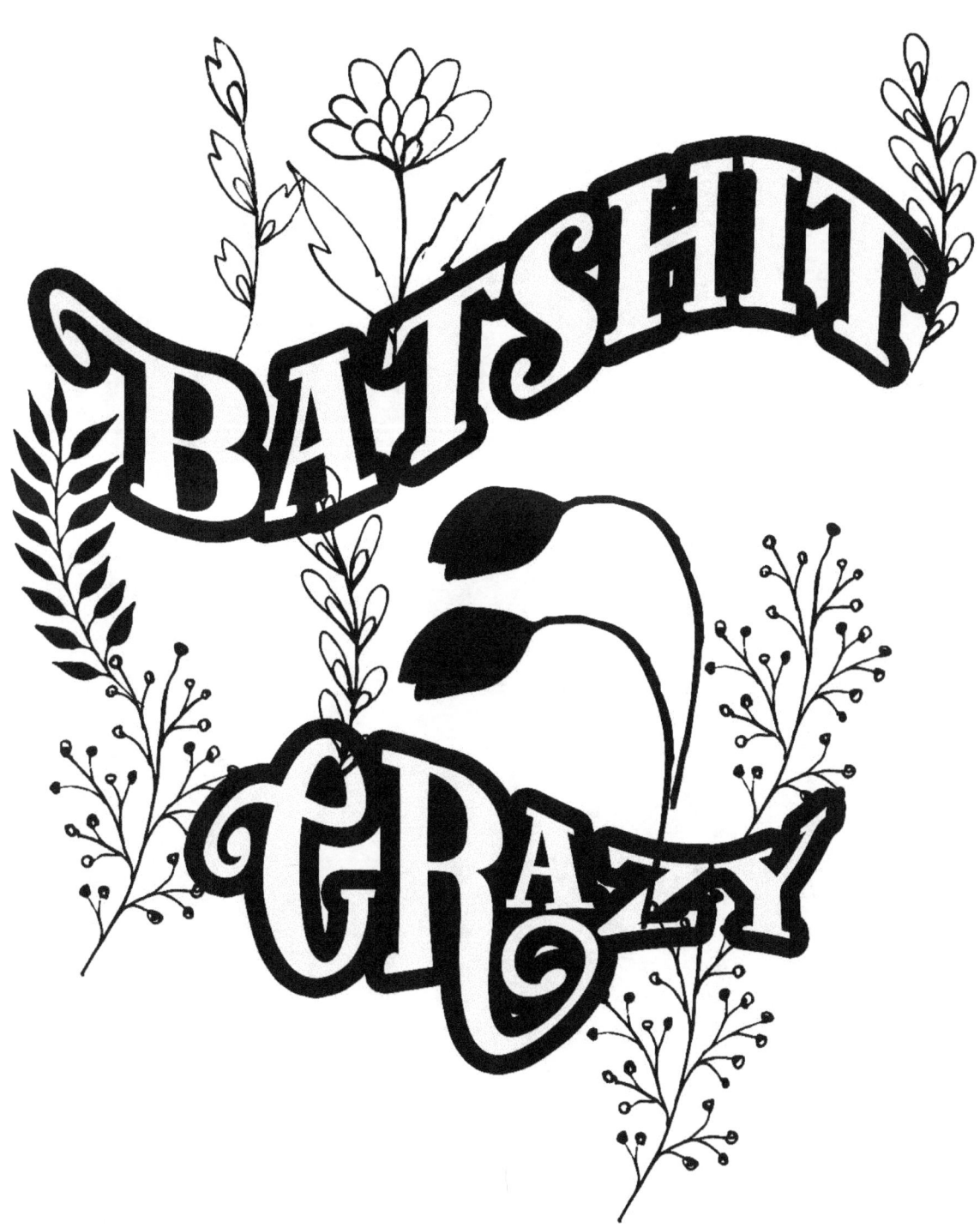

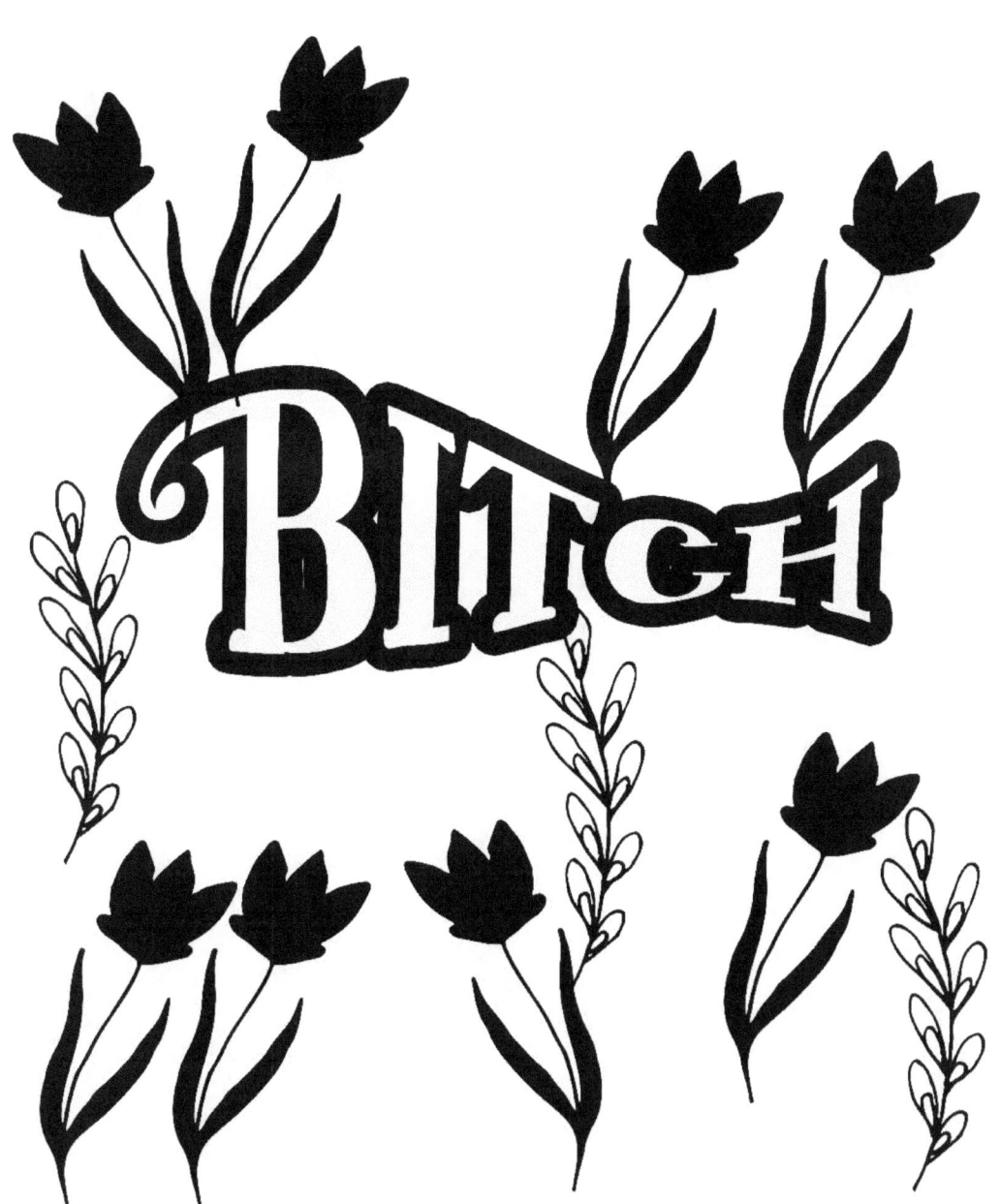

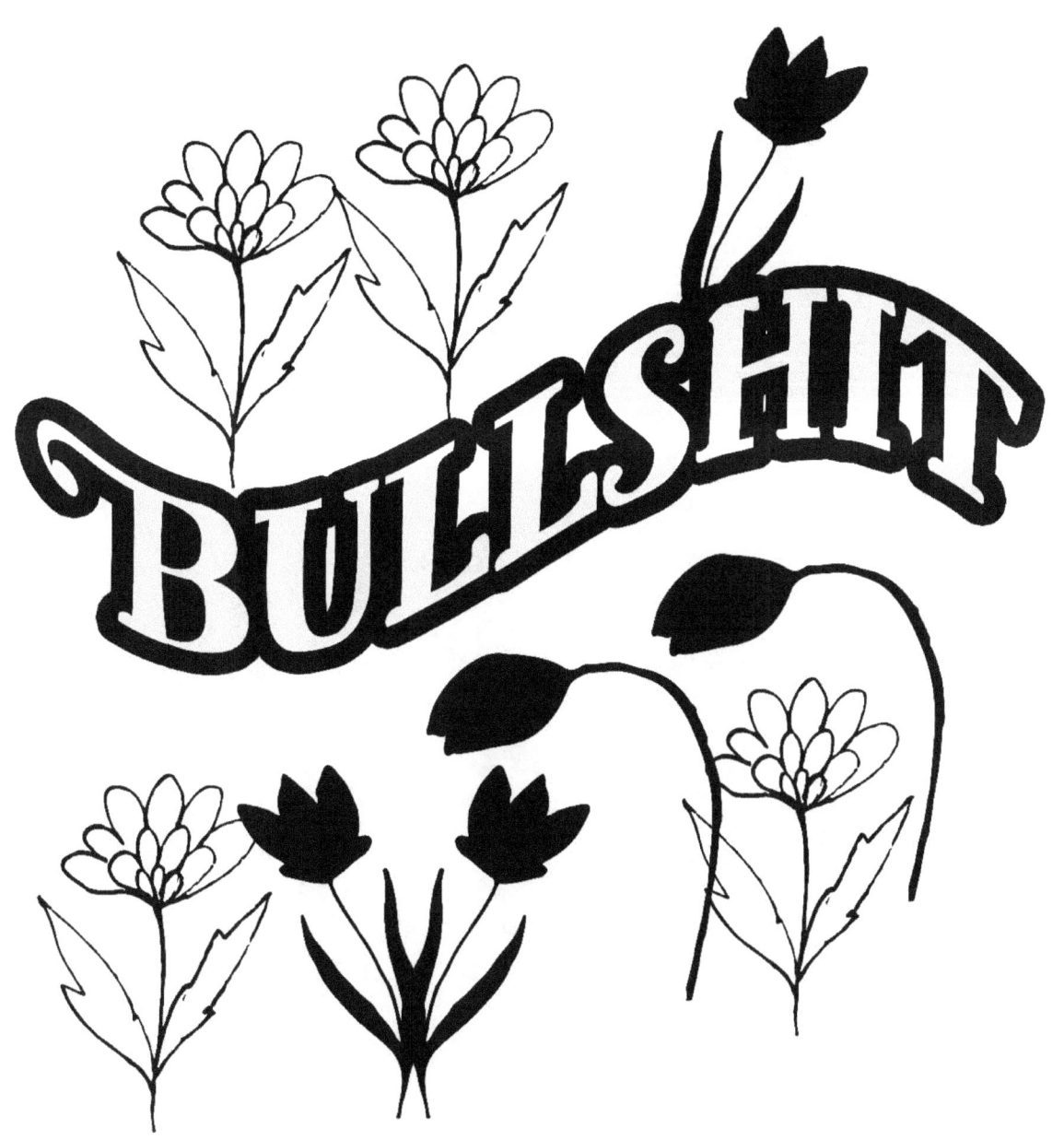

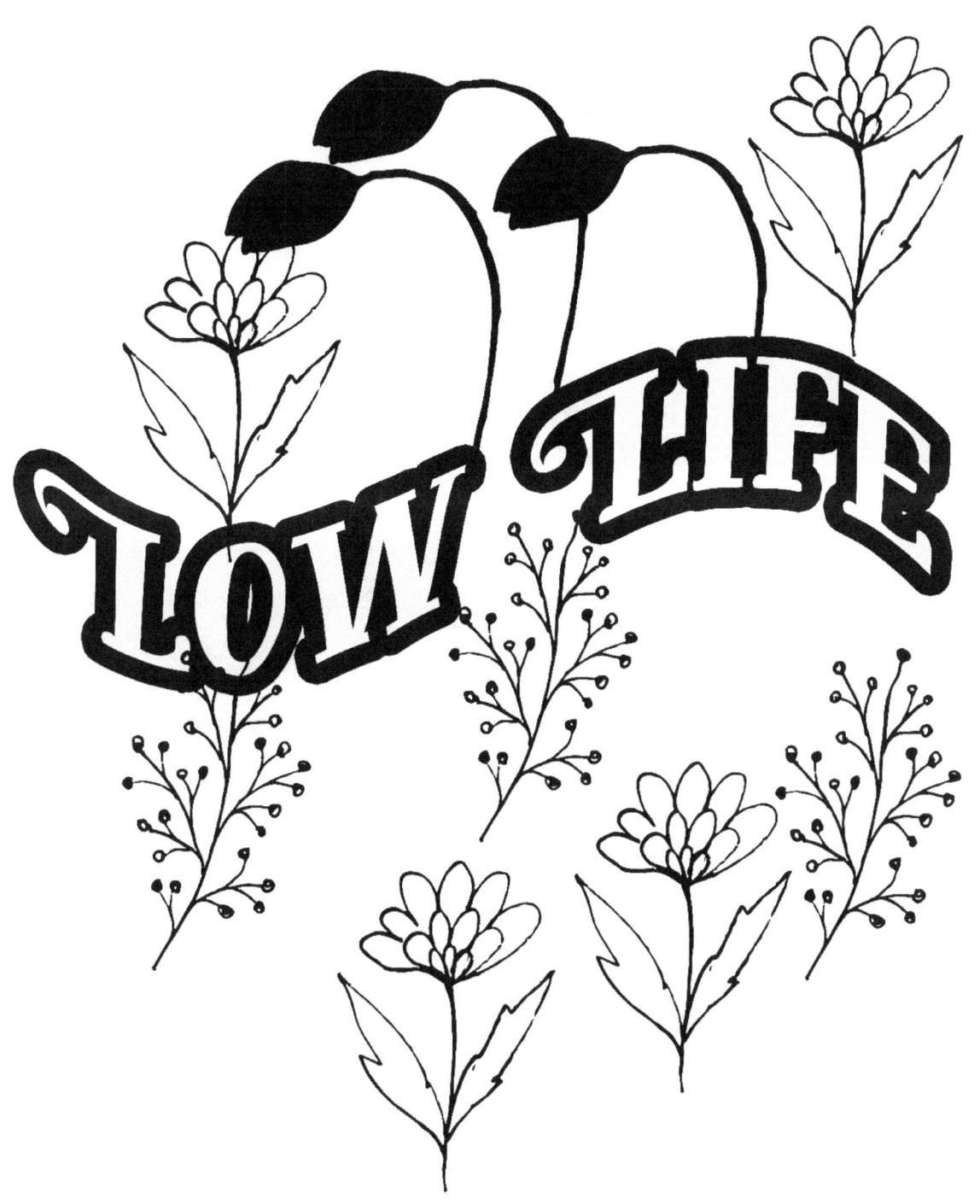

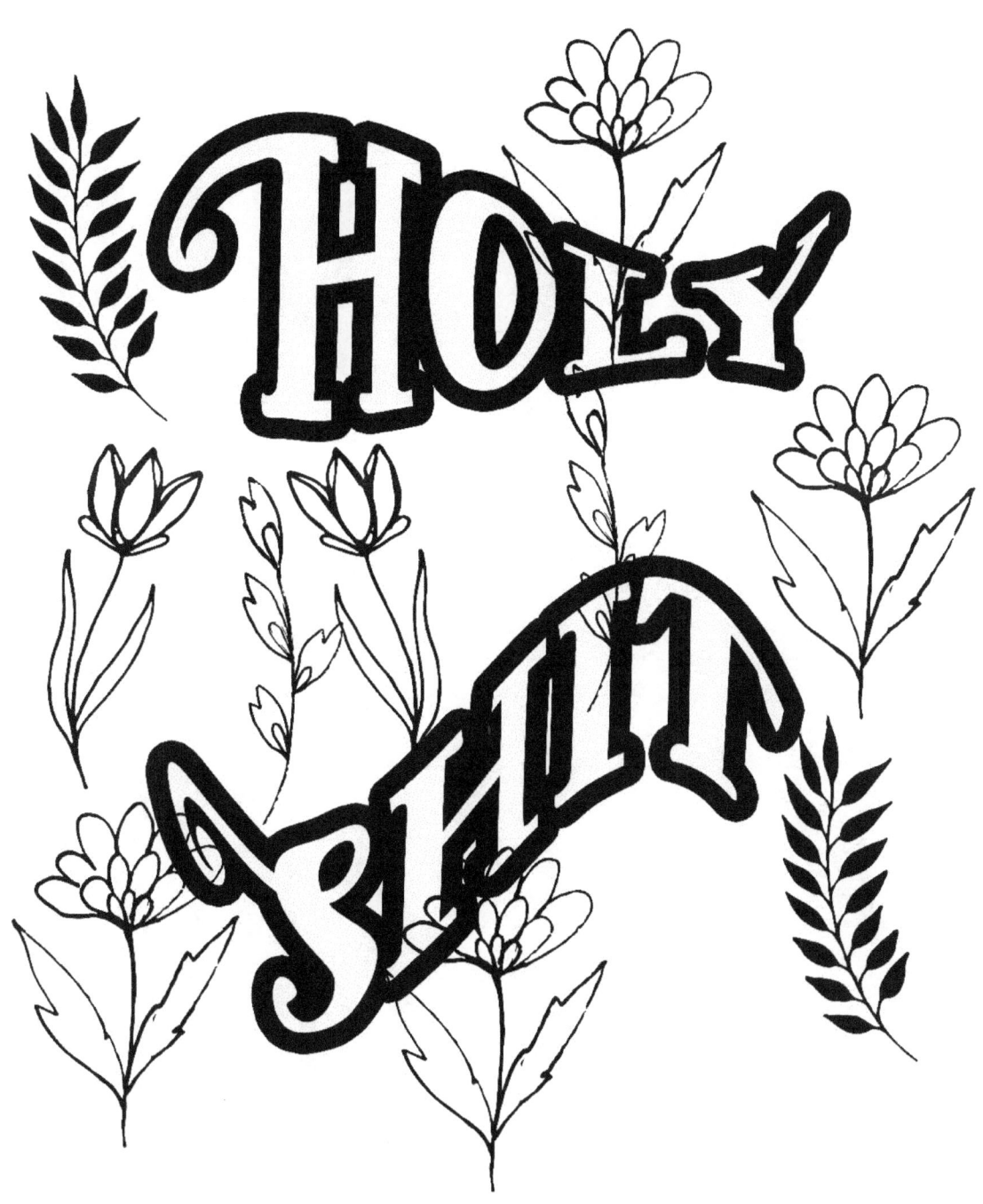

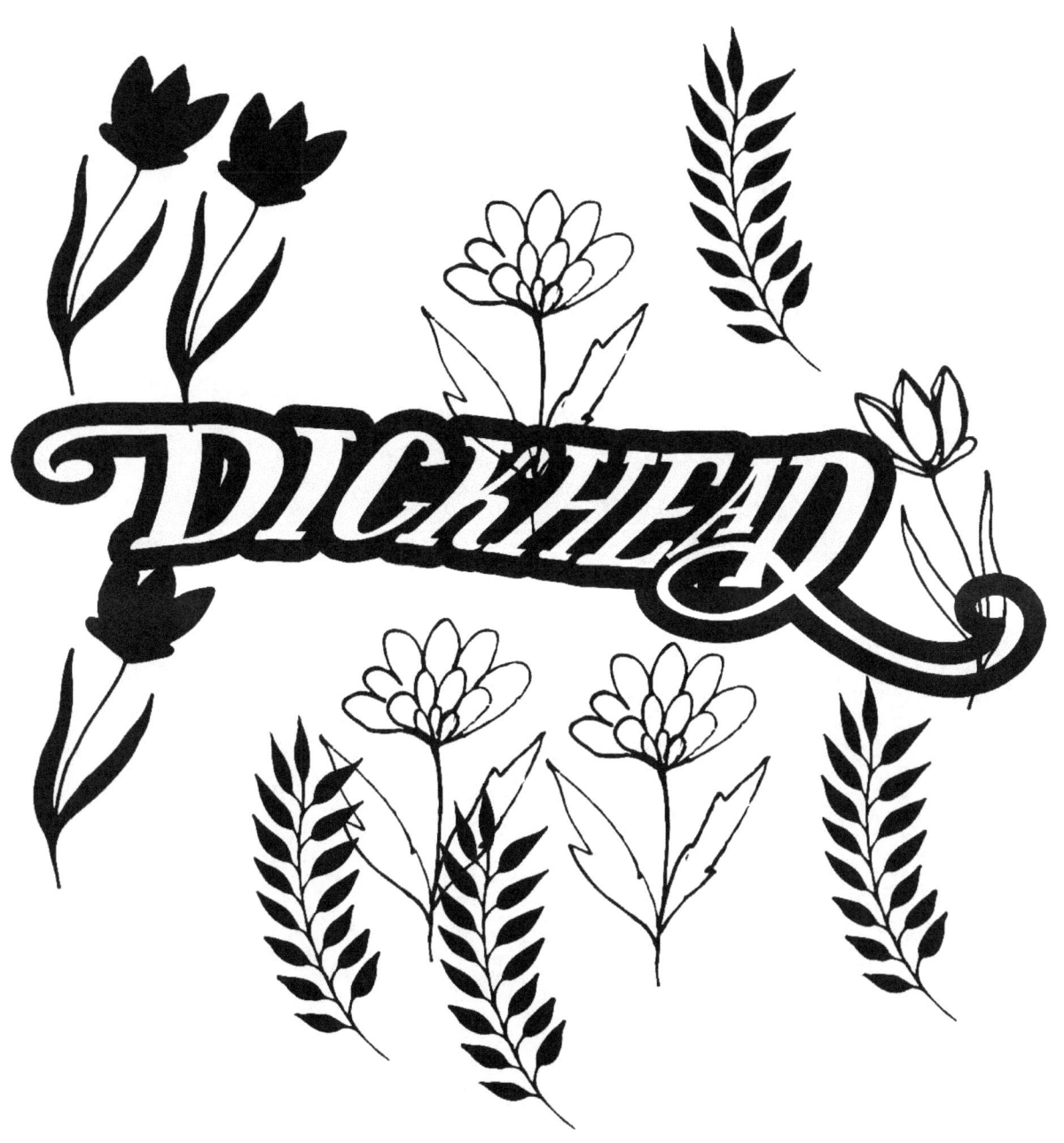

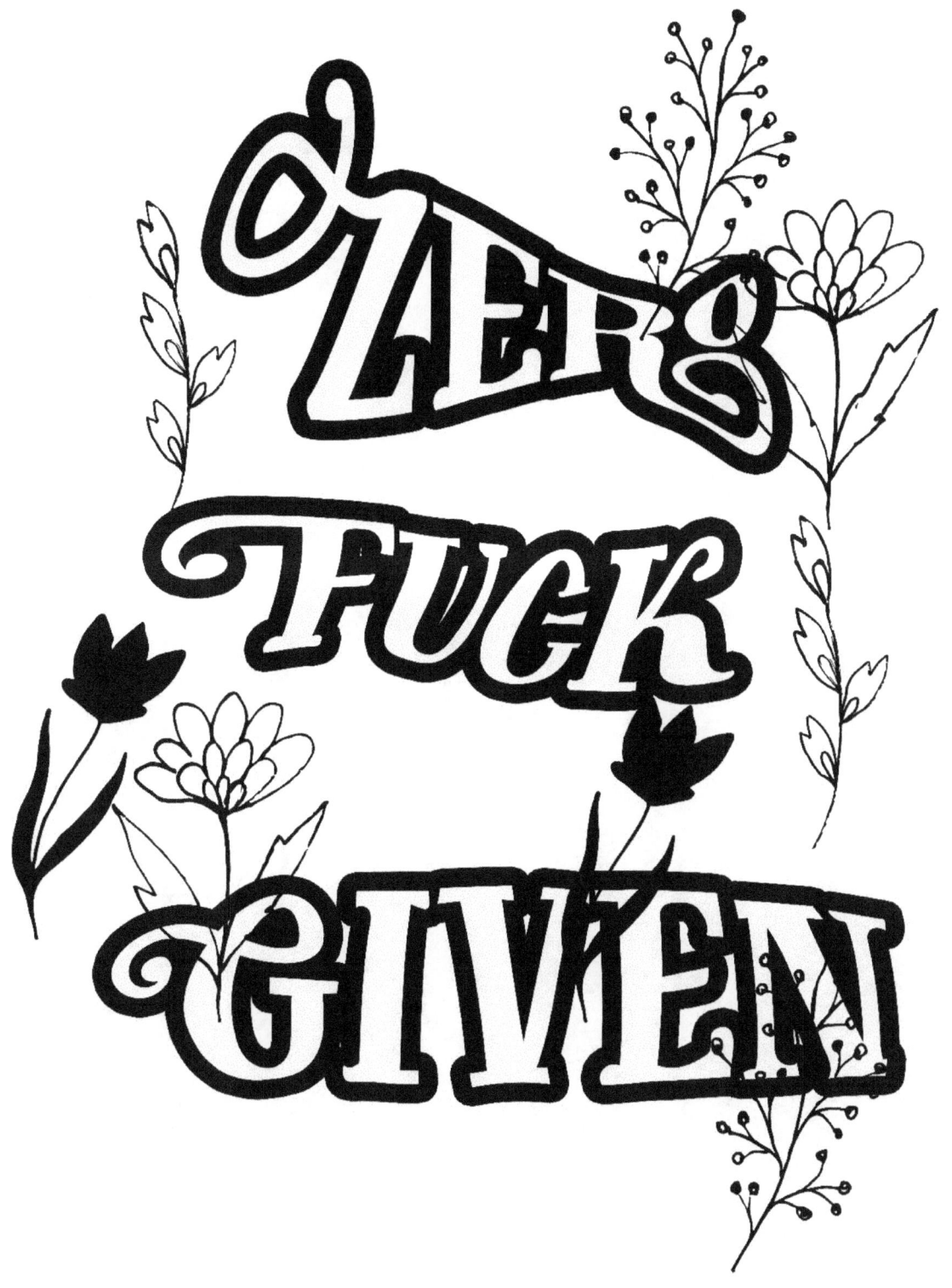

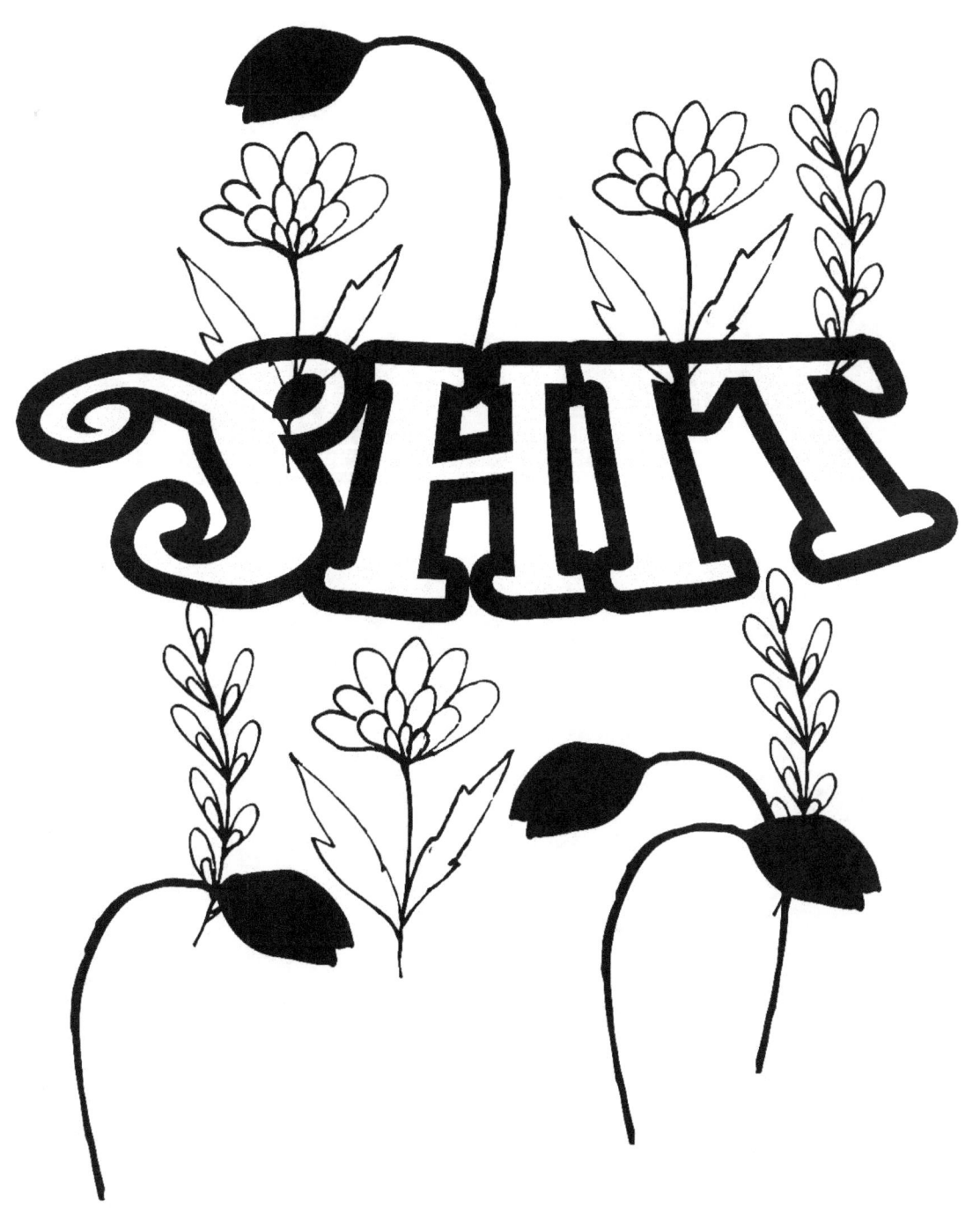

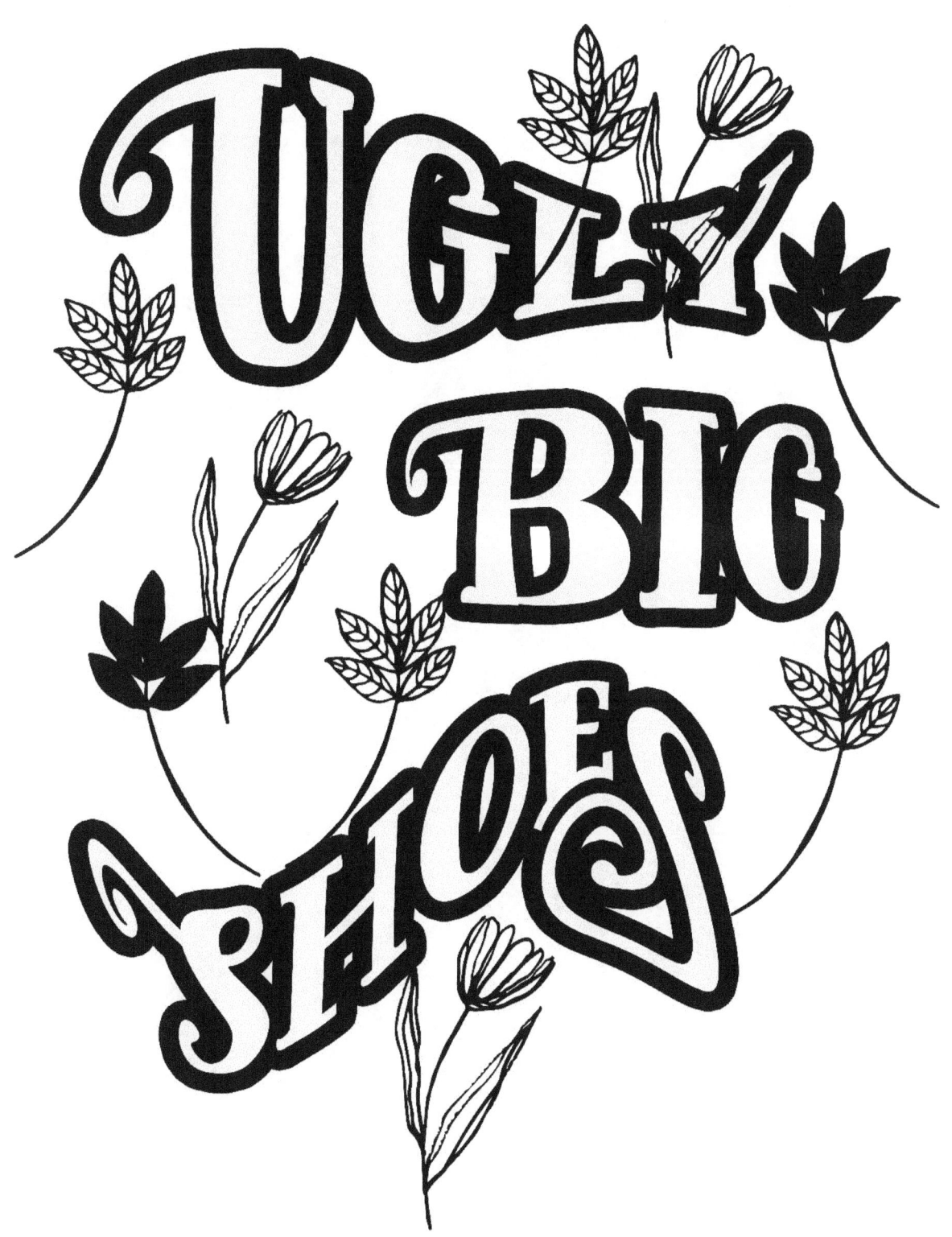

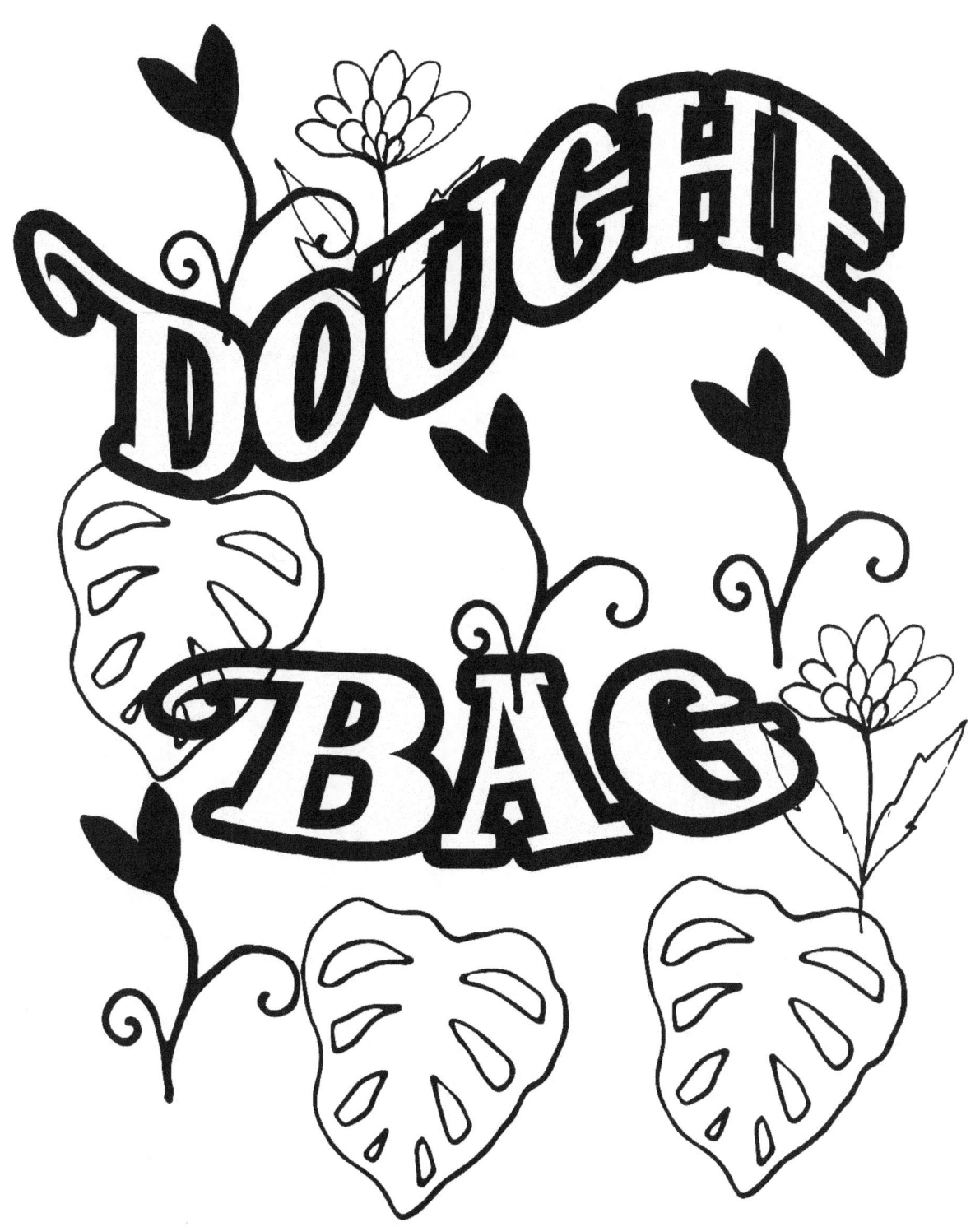

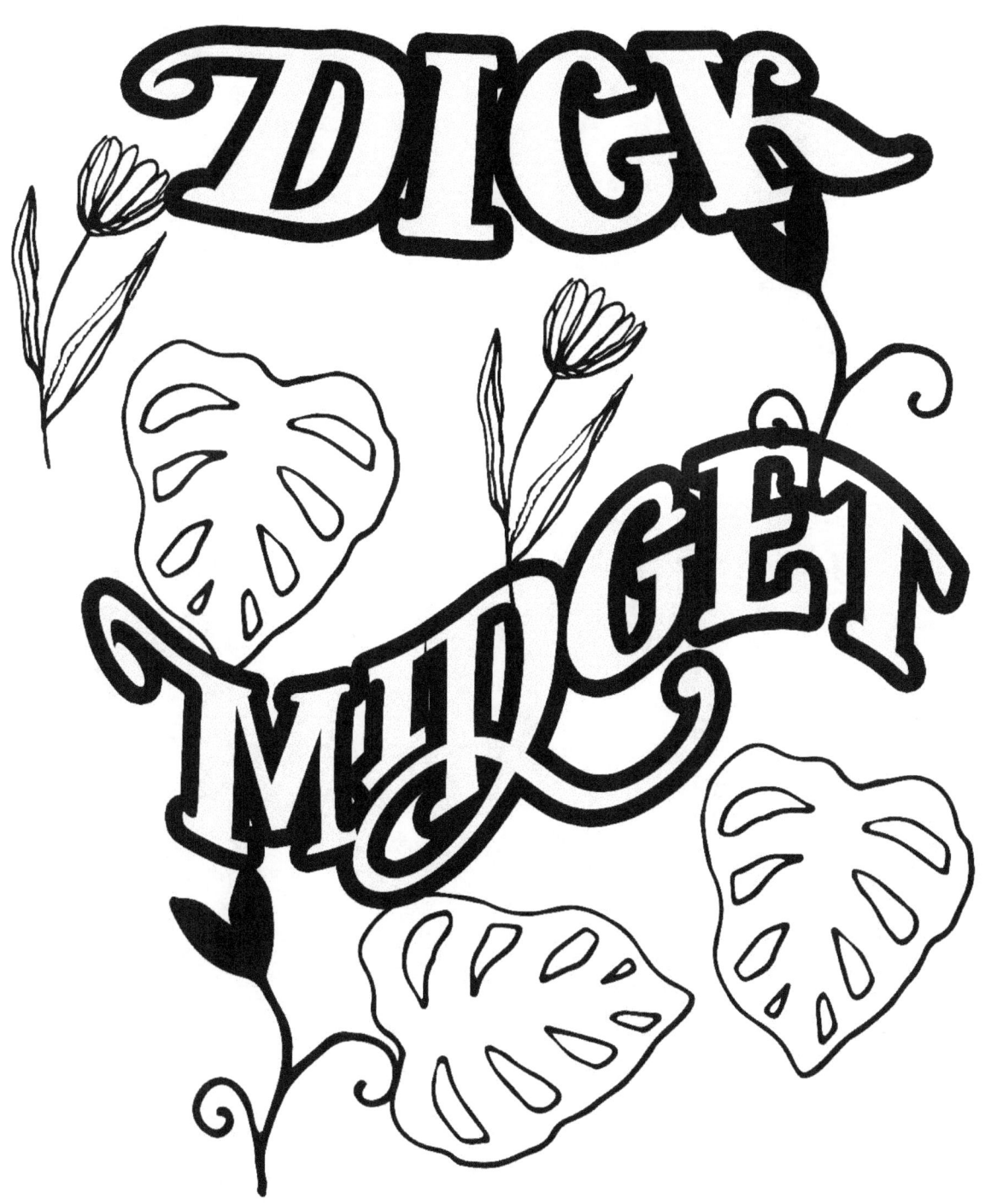

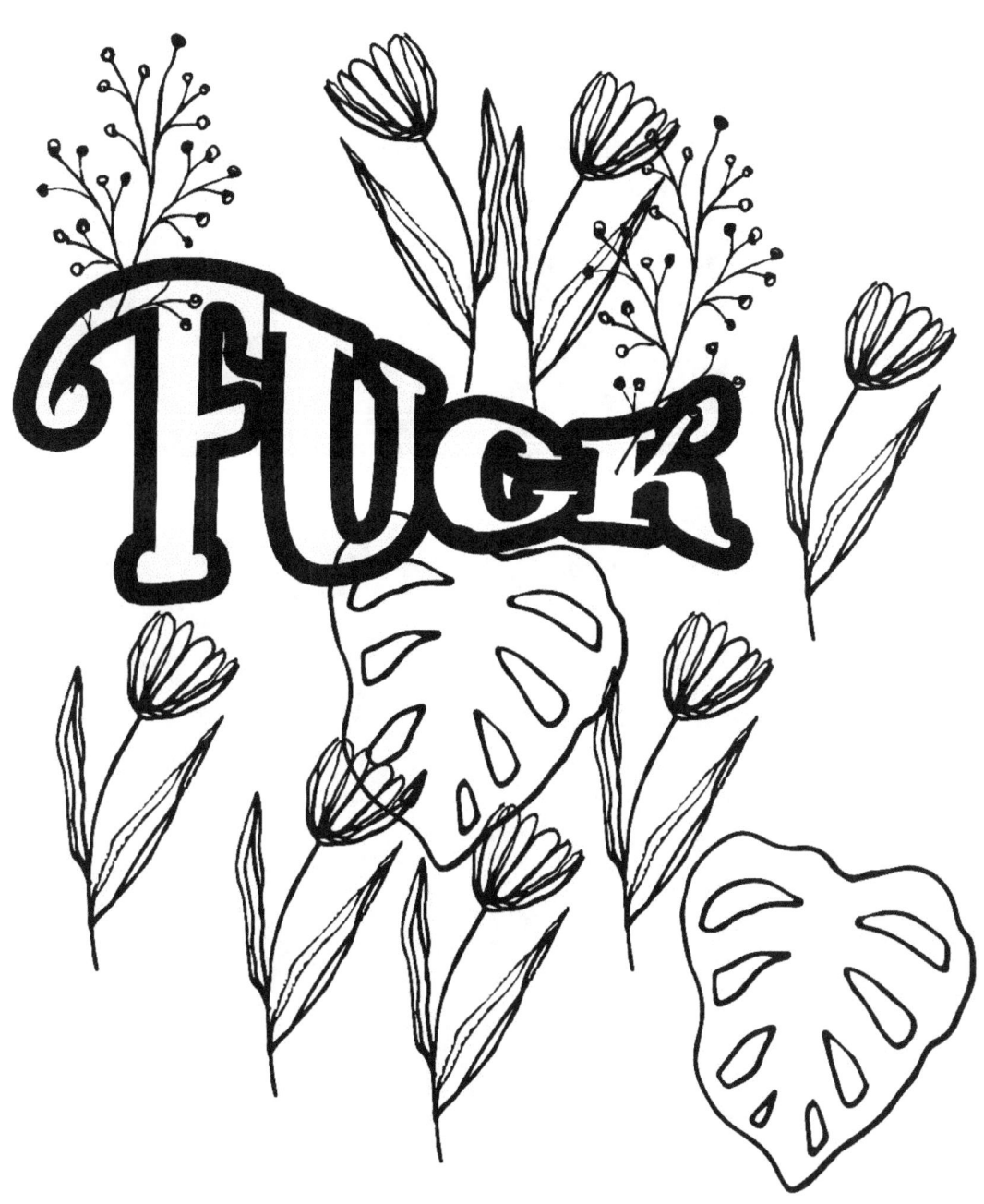

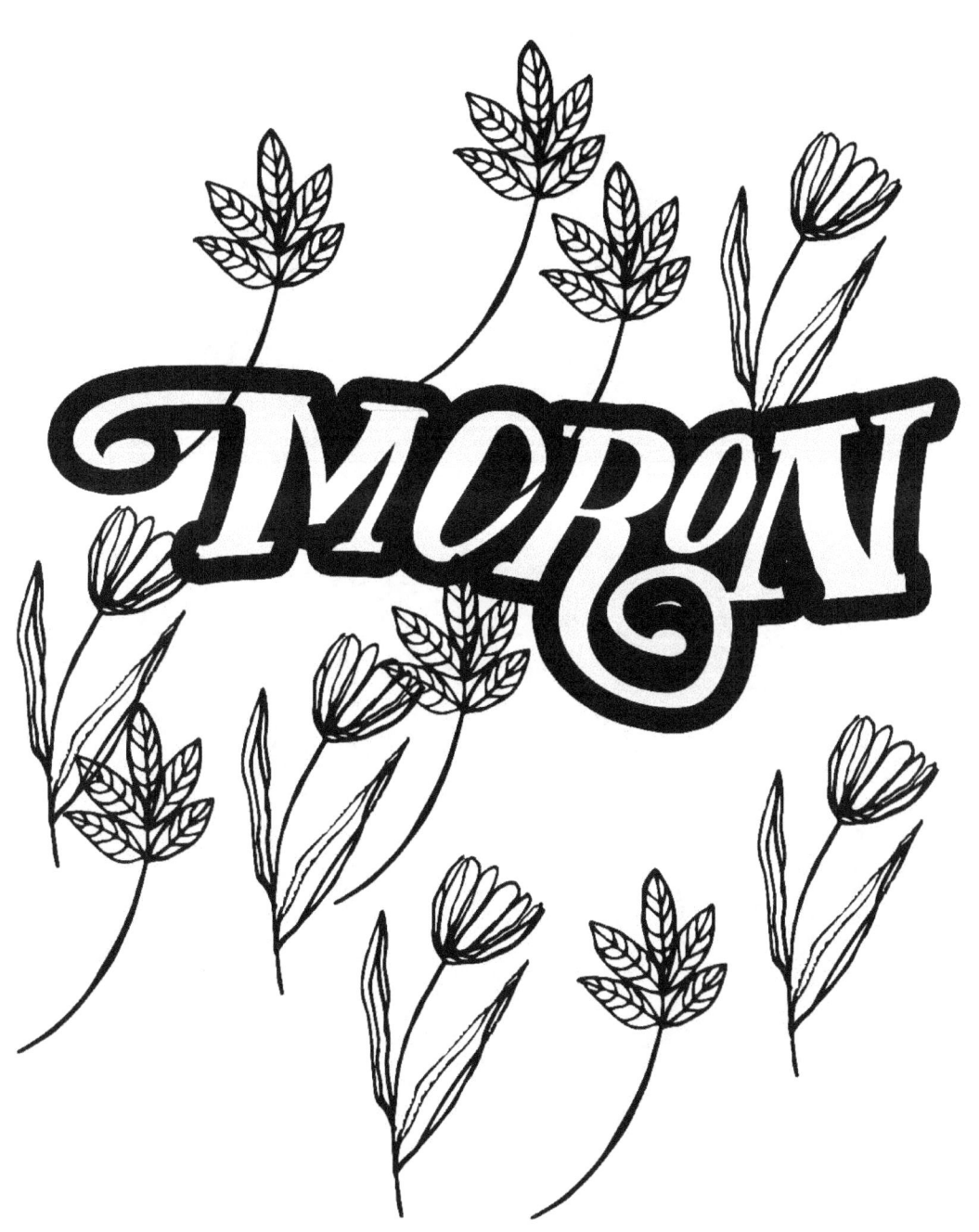

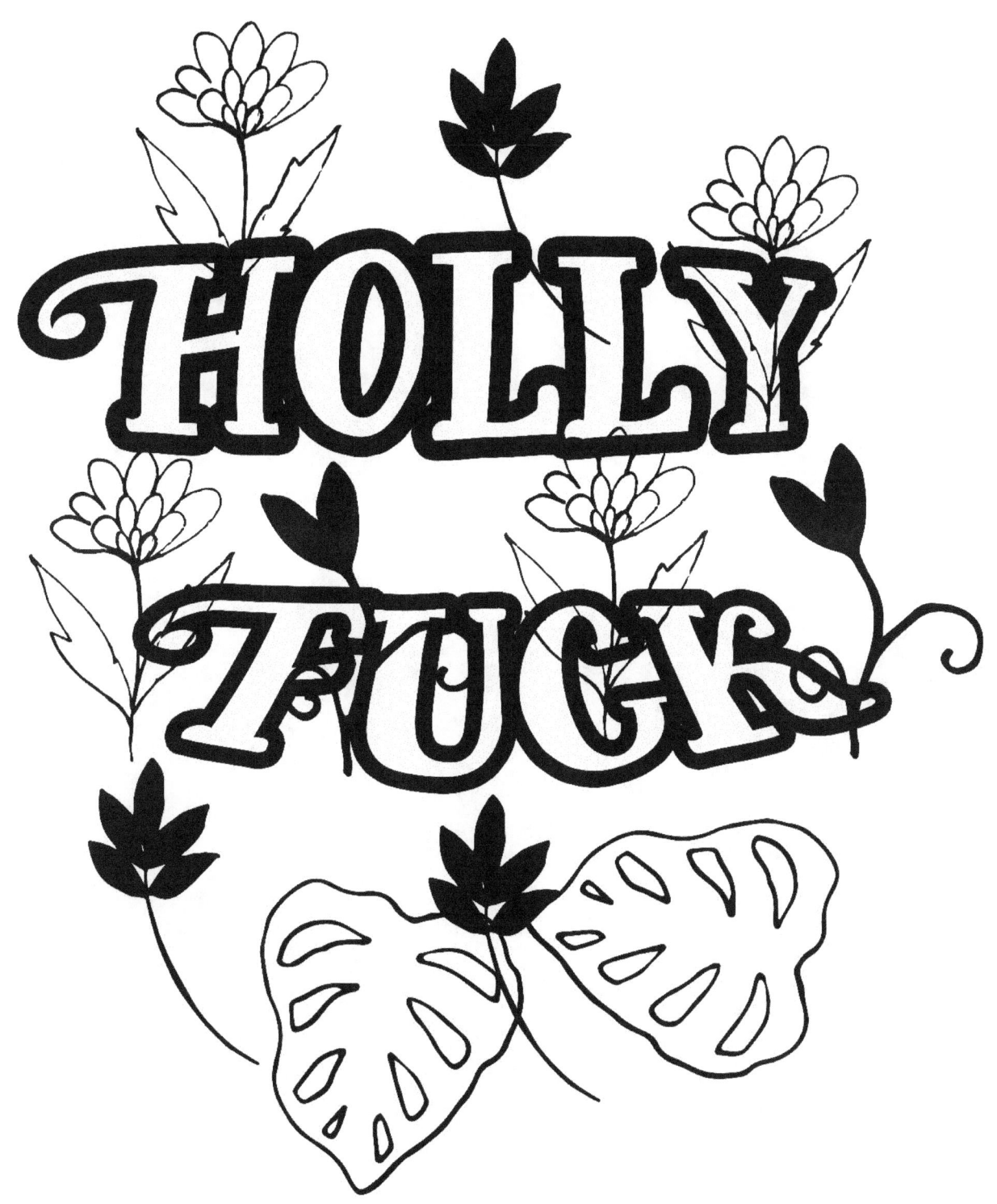

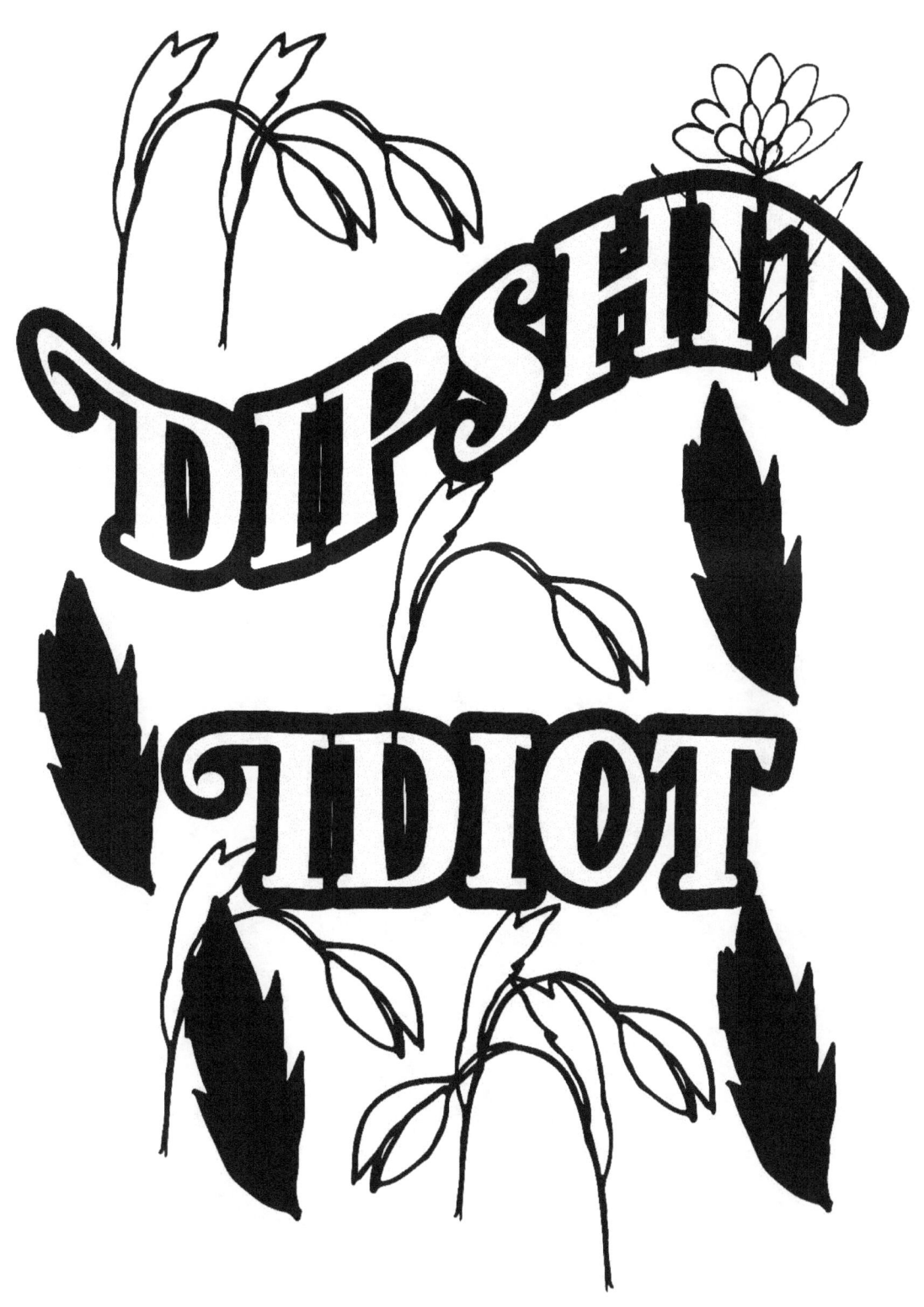

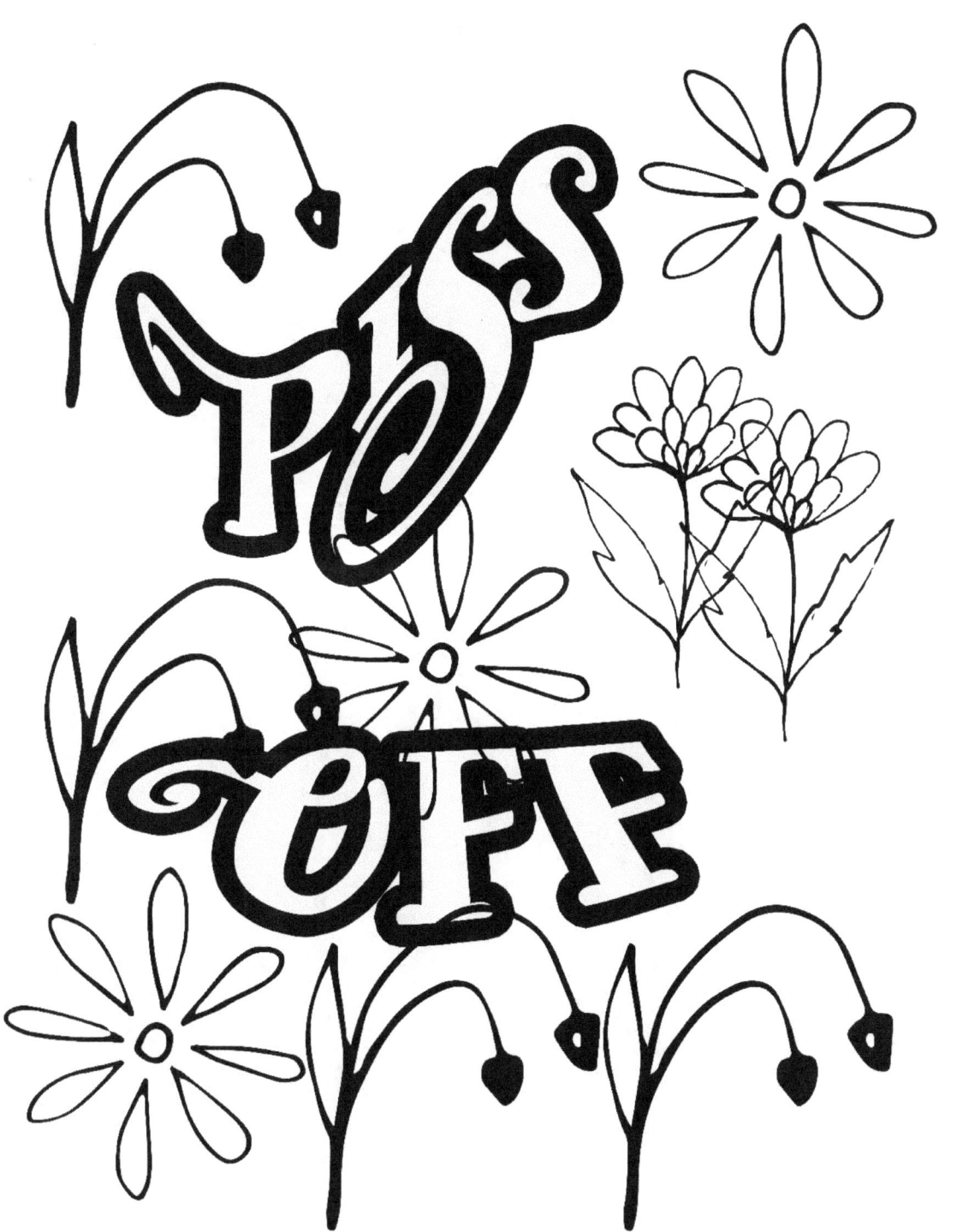

Note

www.ingramcontent.com/pod-product-compliance
Lightning Source LLC
Chambersburg PA
CBHW080638190526
45169CB00009B/3425